Saint G...

Speaks about

Rising Above

A Journey To Higher Dimensions

GORDON CORWIN II

and

SAINT GERMAIN

First Edition

Oceanside, CA. 92056-6237

This Book "Rising Above, *A Journey To Higher Dimensions"*
may be ordered by going to Amazon.com or by visiting the Author's website:
www.SaintGermainChronicles.com
and also through independent and chain book sellers, online retailers worldwide.

The views expressed in this book are conditioned by the Disclaimer which follows. Certain
stock imagery © Dreamstime.com., 123RF.com and Gordon W. Corwin II.

Rising Above

A Journey
To Higher Dimensions

❧❧

Books by This Author

THE SAINT GERMAIN CHRONICLES COLLECTION
A Journey Into Practical Spirituality

VICTORY FOR THE SOUL
Relationships That Work

RISING ABOVE
A Journey To Higher Dimensions

ANGER HEALING AND TRANSMUTATION
An Elevation Of The Soul

TRUE GRATITUDE - Quan Yin
An Open Hand Of Love

Gordon Corwin II aka Lah Rahn Ananda *Amazon * www.Saintgermainchronicles.com

𝕾𝖆𝖎𝖓𝖙 𝕲𝖊𝖗𝖒𝖆𝖎𝖓

CONTENTS

❧ INTRODUCTION ❧

Greetings to All Humanity

I speak to you today … revealing the progressive stages of Higher *Dimensional Spiritual consciousness* … all couched in that Beloved part of your Grand Process called Human Enlightenment.

Behold this Beloved path of upward vibrational evolvement of consciousness … starting from the 3rd Dimension onward, … *ultimately* able to deliver a Divinely sourced and purified Spiritual consciousness of the highest Human octave.

I shall describe for you the *integral elements* of each of five Human Dimensions of consciousness, beginning with the 3rd, progressing through the 4th, 5th, 7th and finally the 9$^{th.}$ I shall also make mention of the 10th Dimension for your edification and noting that this rarefied Angelic level is above your *Human* Dimensional pay grade, My Dear Friends.

You need not worry about the interstitial Dimensional spaces between these four primary Human Dimensions, e.g. the 4th Dimension, as these are merely transitional, bearing mixed characteristics of their adjacent neighbors.

So, for your peace of mind and Well-being along your Spiritual Journey into Dimensions beyond, I intend that you dedicated Ones be given this glimpse of the magnificent road ahead before it touches your feet.

Let Me clarify a momentous distinction for you at this opening juncture, My Dearest Ones. This treatise I now transmit is about you Journeying into **Higher Dimensions of Consciousness** *inside your own Personal Universe.*

Also however, it is important for you to know … in addition to this Beloved path of evolvement … lies another Journey of its own … one that wears a different hat.

I Am speaking of certain **Multi-dimensional Human Beings** that possess Inter-dimensional abilities to commune directly with Ascended Masters in the Ethers ... The Angelic Kingdom … and with other Worlds beyond … as Arcturus, Venus, Orion, The Pleiades, and Cassiopeia.

An ability, albeit beginning or advanced, to hear and commune directly with the Ascended Realm of Spirit and Outer worlds … is of which I speak. These Ones, vessels of Spirit thus Blessed, provide a conduit for Masterful energies to be received upon Earth and subsequently delivered to the Human Realm for inspiration, growth, evolvement, *and Rising up to Higher Dimensional Levels*

Lah Rahn Ananda, serving Myself, the entire Ascended Realm of Masters and all Humanity at this very moment of writing, … is one example of such a Multi-dimensional Being, in this case now advanced to One of My Spiritual Earth Partners, … serving Ourselves Above and all Humanity with clarity, Love and surrendered devotion.

Although incarnated Beings such as Lah Rahn Ananda and others in My service are referred to as *'Multi-dimensional Beings'*, … these Beings are also simultaneously traveling their *paths of Rising Above To Higher Dimensions,* each transcending on their own with Our constant care and nurturing.

For Our Multi-dimensional Beings on Earth, their outreach and contact pierces the Veil between Worlds, and enters the Realm of Spirit ... reaching inward to the Ascended Master Realm and further yet into the Cosmos, … into the very core of spinning Divine energy ... Creation itself.

These Devoted Multi-dimensional Ones like Lah Rahn and others in Our service are doing 'double duty'... serving Humanity multidimensionally and Rising Above … all in one lifetime. We Ascended Masters are Ambassadors to the Creator. We embody and gift Divine energies of Love and Wisdom to Our Multi-dimensional Beings … that bring forth to you transmissions such as you now have before you.

Traveling the <u>Multi-dimensional path</u> with Spirit is a most unique process of evolvement ... this time <u>directly</u> linked to communicating as One with Spirit, ... whereas Rising Above, Journeying to Higher Dimensions is a <u>purification and transformation process of your own Personal Universe.</u>

Alright.

Now, a special gift of guidance for you.

<u>A note about the way you read this book</u>. Curious Egos who would read My works will frequently indulge themselves in '*flipping through the pages in random order*'. Often these Ones will read the end before the beginning. As Saint Germain in service of Humanity, I *strongly* advise you to read this book ... and all of My other books ... in the exact page order presented. In sequence.

You may want to double back and <u>re-read</u> certain sections, and this I highly endorse.

However, if you skip around willy-nilly, hopscotching back and forth, you will miss the needed groundworks I lay to understand, or rise to BE the

energies presented in the subsequent parts. This Wisdom is given in a *specific order for your comprehension.*

Harken my words here, My Dear Friends, as resisting this *sequential reading guidance* will leave you confused and possibly disillusioned … with missing parts essential for this Journey To Higher Dimensions. I trust that enlightenment is your objective?

Here is My overall intention. These energies I Am transmitting today are intended to guide and inspire you with uplifted optimism, knowing the possibilities that can Be in your future … as you faithfully and diligently walk along the path of *your individual Grand Process and unique Dharma.*

For Human understanding at this juncture, as I speak *separately of* the *four primary levels of Human vibration,* … the 3rd, 5th, 7th, and 9th, … *know that the higher Dimensions of these are surely attainable by those of you with … seemingly, … Super-human abilities and determination for evolvement in this lifetime.* By gathering all of your means available, I urge you to perceive *this entire journey* upon which you are about to embark as a *grand reward* … in addition to the individual upliftings that you may receive along the way … evolvements that may be *initially perceived as Super-human* but in practice totally possible for the incarnated.

As you graciously move your consciousness up the Spiritual ladder, rung by rung, *honor yourself to fully experience and embrace each level, each individual Dimension that I present here,* … before *grasping at the next rung.* As We proceed together today, you will understand the reasons.

Yes indeed, Human Egos find this journey to be a momentous 'scaling of Mount Everest', … very challenging and often confrontive, ironical and perplexing. Your Ego will need to give itself up!

You will need Our Masterful coaching along the way. You will need to *surrender your Ego to your Higher-self so you can be taught*! You will need to give up your 'Ego's baggage'.   An Ego that believes *it knows* and *is always right* will need to relax its grip on the real You. Are you with Me so far?

Yes, seemingly *Super-human changes are asked of those who* put boots to this road. I Am confident you have the innate capabilities to evolve and shine brilliantly … *if you are honest with yourself and with Spirit and follow Our instructions,* My Dear Ones. Remember, denial and self-delusion will reverse your progress and keep you stuck, replanting you in the Third Dimensional (3-D) c onsciousness that has you by the neck!

> **It may take some years or additional lifetimes of living this 3-D life to realize there is an alternative way of *living and Being* that can afford you an exponential quality of life … one of peace, Love, joy, abundance and much more. Many turn 50 years of Earthly age before reaching this point! You Younger Ones are invited to beat the crowd.** (Master chuckles … …)

Our beloved El Morya will gladly escort you in these *daily Plutonian awareness pursuits of change and progress.* He is Our champion for Devotes to lead *a full-scale Human life,* complete with a maximum possible range of life experiences and 'ah haas' sourced by your awareness, Dharma, Higher-Self and Soul path.

As an *incarnated Human ... living to whatever extent you are in the Third Dimension,* ... you are naturally mingling constantly in this tangled maelstrom of twisted energies, *most of which have been sourced by Mankind itself.* Collectively and individually, this would be You and yours!

As a newly incarnated Human, when you have landed in this Third Dimensional (3-D) destination for reincarnating Souls, ... the complexity of encountering this energy becomes humongous and commonly overwhelming. Let the pages of this Introduction provide you with an insight to <u>consciously</u> *sort things out, the yin and yang, dark and light, and balance those energies that intermingle.*

Portrait Marius fine art

'Circles of Consciousness' follows, giving you a larger picture of events that have developed over the preceding 20 Earth years, for example, and during many preceding Ages.

Use these insights to realistically observe today's current *condition of the 3-D consciousness*, as it stands before your eyes now. If your emotions are triggered, do your best to manage this with ease and grace, ideally being an unbiased, nonjudgmental observer *intaking in what Is* … perhaps with a note of compassion. Your judgements will only serve to block your progress and keep you stuck.

Realize and know as We begin today, that <u>your Journey to Higher Dimensions is **a grand healing process.**</u> You must, at the outset here and now, recognize the makeup of *Earth's 3rd Dimensional secular consciousness* as the mixed pot of energies that it truly Is. *By now you surely experience the brilliant beauty, Love, enjoyment and satisfaction that can be found here if you try, … if you are willing…* willing to transcend the Duality!

And, in sharp contrast to the Light, acutely observe the counterpart lurking in *Earth's Duality* … pounding its way to the forefront in full force. *You have surely experienced the darkness and negativity of Human behaviors inside and around you and yours, … reacting with voracious appetites and actions of disharmony, conflict, destruction, and killing one another to get what you want.*

Consequently, in your approach to this *Journey of the Dimensions*, it is paramount that you know what needs to be healed ... before you try to heal it! *Yes or Yes?*

You need to heal the way you deal with the Duality that resolutely sits front stage center at this point.

In ALL Dimensions I portray here, your primary healing task is to replace Duality with Non-duality in your Personal Universe. Non-duality then transcends darkness that nonetheless will continue to posture in the 3rd Dimension itself. Be clear, **attempting to crush the dark side of Duality in the World is not your task.** Duality has been created as part of the 3-D.

Tattoo this into your consciousness, mind, body and Soul ... before you read one more of My words here!

Healing the way you interact with Duality pervades throughout this entire Journey, Folks. There are no shortcuts, no excuses, no arguments. This is a simple TRUTH.

All progressive stages of this *Journey to Higher Dimensions* highlight Duality healing ... in one degree or another ... changing from abruptness in the 3rd and 5th Dimensions, to more refined and subtle changes in the 7th Dimension, ... before *arriving and Being the energy of the 9th.* Re-read this and the forgoing 2 pages before you proceed. It will give you a firm foothold for cliff climbing ahead!

CIRCLES OF Consciousness

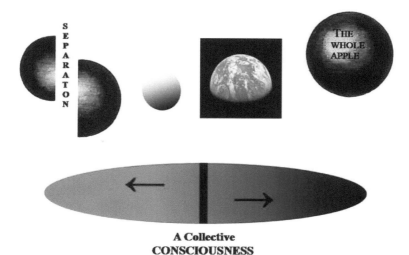

S
E
P
A
R
A
T
O
N

THE
WHOLE
APPLE

← →

**A Collective
CONSCIOUSNESS**
In

Integratiion OR Disintegration

☺

Divine Law
Universal Law
Unity
Peace
Love
Co-operation
Win—Win
Harmony
Blessings
Grace
Abundance ↑
Joy

TRUTH

**Collective
And
Individual
EGO BEHAVIOR**

Ego always right
Domination
'Me First'
Subjugation
Abuse of
Power
Greed
Conflict
Fear
Disorder
Combat ↓
Distruction

**INDIVIDUALS OF
HIGHER VIBRATION** AND

CONNECTED TO SPIRIT

EGO-DOMINATED

INDIVIDUALS

 hich circle is knocking at your door?

Saint Germain

Through
Lah Rahn Ananda
10-20-2008

The starkly <u>divided Third Dimensional</u> energies you see before you, here and now today, are *the consequential handiworks of Ego behaviors and unaligned uses of Free-will choice.* Can you recognize this? Listen to your 'news' *if you dare.*

Nonetheless, within this Third Dimension (the 3-D) is where most of you live. It is in place such as it is, … like it or not, … and its still your job at the outset is *to accept the '<u>Is</u> of What Is'.*

Know however, this picture you see is not the end. It is only the beginning. Be comforted to know that as you raise your vibration and access the 5th, 7th, and 9th Dimensions, *<u>**your own evolving Personal Universe**</u> will maintain its own integrity <u>amidst other energies.</u> As you progress, your Personal Universe will learn to modulate these mixed energies and house them, all the while keeping you at the level in which you reside at the time.*

As We begin together this fine day, let Me interject some clarity that will span your entire Dimensional Ascension process.

Experiencing emotions throughout this inter-Dimensional journey is not unusual... they will continue to flood forth as long as you are incarnated. Yes, they continue for 9th Dimensionals as well, however here they are *Masterfully processed in microseconds with ease and grace.*

As you walk this Dimensional path, ... the ways you react and process your emotions will need to progressively change.

The highlight of this modulating process will show you the aligned and enlightened way to process and manage your emotions ... a dramatically change for the better ... into increasingly higher modes of aligned behavior ... draining less and less of your vital Chi energies from you mind and body ... as is the case now.

I AM speaking of your manner and *regard for treating the inexorable EMOTIONS* you experience as a Human.

Emotions are sensory gifts, naturally received as an integral part of Being Human. They will flood into your Being in droves, and you need to accept this as 'part of your Human package'. By your choices, Emotions can be allowed to 'trigger' you into detrimental unaligned behaviors or they can be Masterfully managed to enhance this process of Raising Up your vibration through the Dimensions … with new behaviors about which I shall now speak.

You can choose to embrace your Creator's design handiwork as a gift **or** view it 'a pain in the neck' where you kick and scream, squirm and struggle, negatively react, resist and *become consumed … drowning yourself in your own emotions,* … … as many of you do … *in which case if you continue you will likely remain 'stuck' in the lowest of Dimensions I shall describe here, … and that would be the 3rd Dimension.*

Now and always, I suggest that you heartfully embrace your emotional energies with *Self-Love-patience* as you proceed on this Spiritual journey of enlightenment.

As you are *Rising Above To Higher Dimensions,* your Highest-Self will begin to abandon those lower vibrations that no longer serve you . . . while you sustain this higher Dimensional ground.

And consequently, with good fortune, those who rub elbows with you may assimilate some of your *higher Dimensional energies you acquire over time.* Light is a

Positive, penetrating and contagious force that can 'go viral', as you would tritely say in the 3-D ... if only you will give it a chance. Read on, My fine feathered Friends.

So far, I have referred to Dimensions 3,4, 5, and 7. *Beyond these lies the Beloved 9th Dimension attainable by enlightened Humans,* ... and beyond that the 10th Dimension... where Our Beloved Angels tread.

Although the 10th Dimension is not accessible for you to reach *while incarnated,* ... for your awareness expansion, I will nonetheless describe this to you in due course here.

My treatise this day is purposefully an oversimplification, I admit, and designed to provide you with *understandable milestones ahead* ... albethey *traversed over several reincarnations, many lifetimes around the Karmic wheel.* Embrace and Grace your own future now ... with Self-Love... and concurrent Self-surrender to 'what Is' *with all of the ease and grace you can muster.*

We shall now individually address these Dimensional energies as:

The 3rd Dimension
A Plane of Hope and Possibility

The 5th Dimension
The House of Higher Healing

The 7th Dimension
A Space of
Liberation and Being

The 9th Dimension
Palace of Purity

The 10th Dimension
Where Angels Tread

Join with Me now as We begin this delightful trek into
Spiritual Dimensions Beyond the Veil.

❧ The 3rd Dimension ❧

A Plane of Hope and Possibility

Here you inhabitants of Earth commonly live in a vibration permeated by Ego, transient energies, and occasional flashes of White Light. The Ego portion sources behaviors that keep you, for the most part, locked in the box of Human illusion, survival, and fear, sprinkled with occasional bursts of kindness and Love. You continuously react to a flood of emotions that desperately need *daily doses of aware tendering, Love and processing. This is where we are going.*

Know that this 3rd Dimension of consciousness serves as a *landing spot for reincarnating Souls destined for and arriving upon Planet Earth.* It is a space of consciousness that many of you have collectively continued to call home for eons of incarnations. And, before you ask, other *Cosmic destinations for reincarnation*, fascinating as these may be to you, will be left to discuss another day.

So most likely, here you are, living in this 3rd Dimensional Earth-school, confronted with countless Ego energies, mentalities that dominate or wish to be dominated, Free-will choice dilemmas, and of course, the Duality itself upon planet Earth.

While We in the Ascended Masterful Realm occasionally observe 3-D *flashes of higher vibrational* behaviors peeking through with Gratitude, … the 3-D predominantly continues to exude miasma and vomit upon itself judgement, opinion, fear, jealousy, survival tactics, competition, domination, pain and much more, in a confusing convoluted quagmire of Humanity.

Many choices *and resulting energies you create* in this

Dimension are commonly instigated by *unaligned emotional responses and illusions.* Much of this is sourced by reeling emotional patterns … *that repeat unlearned lessons* for centuries, eons, … of recorded Human history and beyond … placed in the Akash.

And still, to be fair and equitable, there has been notable and remarkable 3-D progress in the fields of art, literature, education, medical science, and technology, much *for the greater good of Mankind.*

I would particularly note the discoveries of electricity, healing medical practices, stored program digital computers, your internet communication network, exploration of near and far space, and much more.

Can you also see how your technological advances have surprisingly outstripped and eclipsed your meager advancements in evolution of Human consciousness, both individual and collective? Ponder this question!

Human progress of technology continues to *repetitively advance, seeking the next level of progress, ... although certain Ages have witnessed temporary regressions.* Despite dark Ages, ... do you believe Humanity will ever *revert* to the horse and buggy for transportation in place of your electric cars? So then, what about the progress of Human consciousness? Alright, stay with me here. Why, while your technology bolts forward, does Human behavior insist on *repetitively reverting*, over thousands of years of recorded history, ... *to identical prior destructive 3 -D behaviors* such as I just enumerated, leading to your wars and mass genocides?

What evidence do you see of lasting Dimensional Ascension progress in your ranks or in the Earth World?

Certain 3-D Lessons may have been learned, and yet sadly forgotten. Check your history books, Folks. Read today's Earthly newspapers. Extrapolate these patterns into your individual consciousness ... what do you see? What more must I speak or write to convince you that your 3-D consciousness, collective and more often than not individual, ... is STUCK in survival and darkness? You, as an individual, bear your fair share of the responsibility for the stagnated status quo, as well as for the future *potential of evolvement*, Folks. This Truth may be sobering to those of you who are gaining awareness!

❦

Earthlings were tested early in the evolutionary Earth chain to see *how they would individually and collectively choose to use their gift of Free-will.*

The outcome of these choices, individual and collective, is what you now see as the 3rd Dimension.

To all but the numb, this should be sobering!

Many before you have heard the wakeup call and *individually taken action to evolve your individual consciousnesses.* Congratulations to you. You are the Light carriers.

We Above pray that individual enlightenment will soon spread to your governments upon Earth! I implore you, here and now, to be a part of a potential mass upward trend and movement of energies. Given sufficient individual impetus, this trend can influence the collective healing into the Dimensions you are now reading about!

❦

Choices and resulting *energies you create* in this Dimension desperately need purification and refinement, beginning in this plane of Hope and Possibility. This treatise is about launching you on a new path upon this plane.

As we start, be honest about the impact of your Free-will choices in the past. *Unwise choices have frequently reflected behaviors of unlearned lessons ... however, in higher Dimensions which We will explore together,*

... the Wisdom of <u>Life's lessons learned</u> will manage to be indelibly ingrained and permanently recorded without escaping. Knowing this should be refreshing to you. This is a trait of Mastery.

My earlier teachings through My Lah Rahn instrument that serves you and Me this day, ... have offered books of <u>interconnected Wisdom</u> and training in Mastering your Emotions.   Do you know that many of your emotional reactions today that lack this Wisdom are keeping you stuck in this 3rd Dimension, locked in the box? Lifetime after lifetime?

I urge you to seek out and find My collective teachings on your own and integrate them with those of today in Rising Above.

My published book 'The *Saint Germain Chronicles Collection'* highlights impactive choices and wise handling of your flood of incoming emotions. You would be wise to add *this treasure trove of Wisdom to your Spiritual toolbox.*

<u>The way you choose to process these</u> *Ego emotions* greatly affects your vibration level ... and with My Wisdom in your corner, consequent openings to RISE ABOVE will appear, Folks. Let Us continue.

<u>Ego Favorites</u>.

Here now for your clarity is just *<u>a short list of 'old time Ego Favorites'</u>* that need your attention. Just per chance, ... do you recognize any as yours? *In the 3rd Dimension, emotions can rattle you and keep you trapped ... unless you have a method to put them into perspective and modulate them into alignment.*

Your Ego can willingly charge into the forefront, …
armed with opinions, anger, revenge and getting even,
denial, being right, greed, judgements, … and around
We go again, Folks!   Sound familiar?

**At this point in My transmission, I caringly
reinforce *the Divine Truth that Human emotions
are a naturally occurring part of Being Human.* In
and of themselves, … contrary to prevalent
common misunderstandings, … Emotions per se
are not meant to be shunned, feared or to be
judged as 'bad' nor 'good', … <u>they simply 'are'.</u>
<u>For your Wellbeing,</u>
*<u>Tattoo this into your skull, once and for all!</u>***

Be aware when red-light flashes of misunderstanding
about emotions appear and blind your vision!

<u>How you process your emotions </u>is another conversation
to follow. *In addition to My words today, c*onsult My
book "<u>Anger Healing And Transmutation, *An Elevation
for the Soul"*</u> Gordon Corwin II   Amazon … for
additional guidance and processes to Master your
emotions and anger. <u>You will need this</u> constructive
guidance for Dimensional Ascension.

Once you cross this hurdle, your process in motion will move forward in earnest. Otherwise, kindly re-read the foregoing pages until this Truth becomes a permanent part of You!

Now, more about processing emotions.

In brief, *wise processing of Emotions* will ideally begin by an instantaneous awareness that they are present.

Emotional entry points can show up as mental, physical and sometimes both, in one sequence or another. Have you noticed?

• Then … you are at a crossroads. Do you make tempting, perhaps habitual, choices to indulge in Ego reactions … or not … OR rather, do you consciously catch yourself and *alter any negative perspectives into a neutral emotional zone, better yet, ideally into the positive zone?* This must be done consciously and of your own Free-will ... and learned to become automatic. You need to want to do this and to thereby clear the path to Rise Up!

Thus positioned with awareness and empowering choice, … you have another choice … to recognize the Truth of the circumstance, *dispassionately and without judgements and without any venom that may be flowing ... inside or outwardly.* This is the next part of this process.

Can you not see all or parts of this scenario flowing through your life?

- Next, you have further <u>choices … to regard the circumstance *dispassionately*, to recognize what is, be with the situation, and to call forth a level of compassion and yes,</u> Love ***to arrive at 'The Truth'.***
- *… All of which Were likely not immediately available when the emotion originally struck its mark?* ***Now you have an aligned choice to stand upon!***
- *At this point, a rational adult conversation can lead **to possibilities for win-win solutions**.*

Perhaps you could re-read the foregoing page or more and ponder it a bit.

A full and complete *treatise on this process* is written in My book: 'Victory for The Soul, *Relationships That Work',* Gordon Corwin II, Lah Rahn Ananda, Amazon …presents Wisdom and processes to learn positive Ego management techniques leading to ...

'The Truth' and 'win-win' solutions in your life. This ability Mastered, qualifies you to Rise Up to these new heights of Spiritual Dimensions I speak about.

Again, I suggest you avail yourself of this *'Victory For The Soul '* book of relationship and Cosmic Wisdom as a part of your *Journey To Higher Dimensions. As you will find, this all ties together with a bow of joy that awaits you.*

<u>With practice, patience with yourself and determination, … your abilities to successfully process and modulate emotions, judgements, opinions, etc. etc. will</u> *escalate into*

the higher Dimensions which follow, … beyond belief! And thus the quality of your life!

In your relationships of *all types*, *some of you are already aware of the joy, Love, Oneness and healing* that can be experienced with flashes of ease and grace.

Others, wishing to remain in a lower vibrational Ego-bound personal universe, will continue to plod, and plow through your 3-D relationship antics … simply *reacting,* *coping and hoping,* … *devoid of actions for healings.*

Good News.

The time required to process Emotions that could have otherwise kept you stuck in the 3rd Dimension … can become progressively shorter, sometimes diminishing to a few microseconds versus hours and days or years it requires in the beginning! Can you relate to this scenario?

If you Master the discipline to carry out My instructions, … in the 3-D and beyond, you will launch forward like *the rocket of evolvement* you are meant to be, My Dear Ones.

What We are about this day is to guide you along a *new and enlightened path*, one in sharp contrast to that of common 3-D behavior. This path would aim to *imbed learned life's lessons, ... Mastered in your aware consciousness and therefore not destined to repeat the stagnant pattern of Human history.* Are you with me?

Yes, *certain fortunate 3-D vibrations* are also intermittently mixed with Love and joy, I must hasten to say, *although 3-D unconditional Love is present at rare times and rationed sparingly.*

The very beauty of Planet Earth itself which houses the 3-D must, of course, be given sterling recognition, honoring and exalting God's miraculous creation of Humanity itself, and the Animal and Plant Kingdoms in residence.

Dark and Light also decorate, by Divine design, your 3-D stage on Planet Earth.

It offers opportunity and hope to awaken *actions of self-realization* that can lead to *aligned Free-will choices* of grand consequence down the line.

Duality

Aligned Free-will choices are part of the Sacred fabric that wraps your individual Dharma.

Beware that *Duality is mingled with ALL Dimensions* of consciousness on your Earth plane.

Your Human gift of Free-will choice is constantly tested and tamped by this Earthly energy of Duality, as you may have noticed?

In the arena of Human life, One can easily choose *Light over dark ... or choose Ego indulgence as the opposite, a*

> **Your degree of Ego indulgence will <u>directly</u> affect and influence the need for countless re-incarnations, ... or on the bright side, choosing non-Duality and the lack of Ego behaviors will affect your *eligibility to move up to the next Dimension, a Spiritual promotion that you can deeply cherish at a Karmic level.***

perplexing dilemma for the uninitiated, of which you must be forcefully aware by now!

And now comes *'The Truth'* interacting in the 3-D.

With your emotions and triggers in full check, you will be greatly assisted in getting to 'The Truth'. Once again, I refer you to this Wisdom I have brought forth in "Victory For The Soul, *Relationships That Work"*, *Gordon Corwin II, Lah Rahn Ananda, Amazon 2022.* I shall not here repeat this already delivered treatise about seeking and utilizing the 'The Truth' ... and working through your emotions and triggers. Your choice to dig deep for your Victory of the Soul or languish in the status quo.

Once you have this book in your possession, I highly suggest you heartfully *ingest the Relationship coaching* … it directly applies to the Ego cleansing you need for Rising Above.

Arriving at 'The Truth' requires Ego cleansing indeed,

Self-honesty, and often compassion, … to gain 'Win-win' relationship solutions. Understand that relationship with yourself is primary, … inside your Personal Universe.

As choices are made, We Above observe a common Human behavior of avoiding the 'Truth' in favor of bolstering Ego sourced opinions, beliefs, and actions, winning, etc. Be alert that this avoidance pattern fosters a stagnation of consciousness, a 'stuckness' that anchors the 3-D resolutely in the mud! Clear recognition of *'what is and what is not'* can guide you handily in gleaning Truth from your life's circumstances and making wise choices. Try it sometime!

Many of you come to Me looking for a *solution* to *extricate yourself* from this lower level of Human drama. Your requests usually ignore 'The Truth' of your circumstance and almost always exclude a desire for 'Win-win' solutions I teach, … favoring the 'I and Me' for a decisive Ego victory. Does this shock you? Welcome to the 3rd Dimension. You would be more shocked at the massive number of Ego-filled prayer requests We Above receive into the Masterful Realm, … daily and hourly. What is your guess about the disposition of these requests?

Your solutions for moving on lie within this treatise, Dear Friends.

Open your eyes and look around your World. Make your choice of Dimensional aspirations!

About judgements. In the 3-D, success is often 'judged' by someone 'winning', 'better than', and achieving the Ego's outcome, with possible prestige, wealth and/or fame somehow connected. As you will soon see, the 5th Dimension of consciousness sources a striking contrast, where *a different perspective of success* comes forth,… imbedding integrity, compassion and fairness, generosity , consideration, and much more.

About resistance. Many of you recognize the triggers of emotions you are experiencing. You also see the resistance to 'The Truth' that shows up in your resulting behaviors. Be assured to know … *resistance to 'what IS' (particularly spurred by your Ego) and to facing 'The Truth' … is overcome and transcended as you progress into the 5th Dimension and higher.*

At this point I AM obliged to paint a picture for you, visualize a bridge that spans the 3-D leading into the 5-D.

Now, behold the forces that keep you on the 3-D side, …
and what it will take to cross this bridge.

HERE ARE 5 STEPS FOR YOUR WAY OUT:

**Open your eyes to this perspective and
you will thank yourself forever!**

*Be forewarned that these following STEPS
may take days or years,
or lifetimes, depending upon you!*

The STEPS which follow must be taken in this order.
Skipping a step will guarantee a setback.

*There are no shortcuts
to enlightenment, Folks!*

Here you shall begin to earn your stripes!

HOW LONG WILL YOUR EGO HOLD ITS GROUND?

our unrelenting and active engagement in the foregoing and the following will move you along your path at lightening speeds, Folks.

This begins the Super-Human part of your journey into practical Spirituality. Laggards and hangers-on *will wonder why they are still stuck…* and yet always have the opportunity to change and regroup.

"Victory favors the bold". Who are *you* now? The choice is yours!

Read on, my fine Ones, your inspiration can intensify as We move through this day.

> *We implore* you to <u>focus intently</u> upon RISING ABOVE this prevailing 3-D lifestyle. Continuous immersion here tempts stagnation of consciousness giving rise to *multiple and countless reincarnation cycles, ad infinitum.*
>
> Note when you *release yourself* from this pit of 3-D delusion … *you create an <u>energetic springboard</u> to use when you launch over that bridge into the 5th and higher Dimensions of* healing that sources Love, harmony and abundance.

Want To Free Yourself
FROM BEING 3-D Stuck?
5 CORE LEVEL steps for your FREEDOM

1.   Fully Realize that your Ego exists. Accept this.

2.   Become crystal clear about what Ego is, about *what* Ego behaviors are versus aligned Spiritual behaviors.

3.   Surrender into a willingness and Free-will choice to CHANGE and give up your Ego behaviors. (e.g., Always Being right, judgements, your precious opinions, arrogance, greed, blaming, dominating, denial of 'what is', avoiding 'The Truth', etc. etc.
See "Tuning Up Your Vibrations" in *The Saint Germain Chronicles Collection* referenced earlier here.)

4.   Take daily positive ACTION FOR CHANGE of your Ego behaviors ... willingly *take correction*; apply *self-correction*; automatically transmute Ego *thoughts and actions* into Aligned Spiritual behaviors. And yes, You will surely need Masterful Spiritual coaching to stay the course. Seek it.

5.   Embrace the fruits of Aligned Behaviors, receive Light from Spirit, maintain vibrational advances, and prepare to hover over the bridge into the 5th Dimension. Be joyful and Grateful for progress!

An extensive portrayal about **'Tuning Up Your Vibrations'**, in The Saint Germain Chronicles Collection, Amazon, is a piece I sent to you years ago through the Instrument Lah Rahn Ananda, that Wisdom still serves you this day.

<u>This same page of Wisdom is</u> *appended here* to provide you with a snapshot of positive *alternative behaviors* that will Bless you in daily practice. *Changing old behavior habits into ones that serve you will open these new higher Dimensional Doors to your delight!*

The needed *Healing coefficient* is not yet fully positioned in 3-D as it is in higher Dimensions. That is why We call it **A *Plane of Hope and Possibility.*** When 3-D Ego energies are modulated, *Soul healing* will gain its momentum. Realizations of Soul connections often gain ground when part of a consciousness flirts with the 5th Dimension and higher.

As you *Tune Up Your Vibrations*, We intend you will be empowered to see flashes of the 5th Dimension come forth into your awareness.

TUNING UP YOUR VIBRATIONS
~ Applied Spirituality from Saint Germain ~

EGO Behavior *compared with* ## Your Highest-Self Choices

"My small story is what counts!" Over dramatizes.
Is selfishly focused, ignoring Unity consciousness.

Ego confuses its small story with Reality!
Indulges in *fear-based behavior,* including anger.

Strives to be "important". The BIG shot! Greedy!

"I'm always right" attitude. Arrogant. Believes
Ego's *opinion* is correct! Ignores Human fallibility.
Re-enforces a sagging self-esteem by denial.

My opinion, i.e., "*my* truth", IS *the* Truth!!!
"There are no other possibilities but mine!"

Self-Aggrandizes. *Dominates* selfishly to
over-ride or restrict others' Free-will choices.
Makes untenable excuses. Projects the blame
onto another one/thing. "It's someone else's fault".
Avoids accountability and responsibility.

Complains about *unfulfilled expectations*.
Demands *immediate* satisfaction!
Prefers *complaining* to implementing solutions!
Gets "stuck" on irreconcilable issues

Obsesses about dissatisfactions.

Escalates frustration into anger and hate.
Enjoys being angry; regards as acceptable!
Impatience accelerates into anger.
Believes anger or hate get the best results,

Uses anger to "bully" others, often hiding *fear*.
Promotes conflict and greed. Seeks revenge.
Unable and or unwilling to *recognize emotions.*

Satisfied staying stuck in Egos's versions
of unlearned life's lessons.

Attached to Ego as a prisoner of its own device.

Overcomes EGO's burning indulgence.
Replaced with *aligned self-choices for
highest good.*
Learns, applies, and remembers life's lessons.
*Embraces this process with empathy and
overshining fear of* change.
Knows Joy through *humility* and helpfulness.

Seeks Truth, applying the merit of different
perspectives to each moment of every day life.
Replaces denial with reality and self-integrity!

Discerns the *difference* between their
belief system and *Universal/ law / Truth.*

Seeks Mastery of Spirit's teachings of Truth.
See The Saint Germain Chronicles Collection.
Knows Truth and accepts reality with Joy.
**Pacifies an untamed EGO into submission
into its rightful role.** Promotes harmony.

Demonstrates patience by shrinking EGO's
stature, now relegated *to take a back seat.*

Seeks out and implements creative
Win-win solutions.
Replaces complaints without squandering energy.
Expresses gratefulness. Sees Blessings!

Utilizes Saint Germain's
healing techniques as presented in His book
'Victory for the Soul, Relationships That Work',
Gordon Corwin II -Lah Rahn Ananda, Amazon.

Recognizes own behavior in real-time.
Elevates negative emotions, raising them up into
Neutral or Positive zones.
Is accountable for Own Behaviors.

**Fully ENJOYS the Mastery and rewards
of Aligned Actions and Higher Dimensions.
Discovers the Human Condition!
Transcends the Human Illusion!!**

Aligns consciousness with Universal /
Divine Law, *freeing their Highest-Self to BE.*

"To Truly Be or not to BE is Your Question". Saint Germain

Through Lah Rahn Ananda 05-2010 Rev. 07/2022

Alright!   Do You see where We are headed?

This objective look at your 3-D and its parts may be a bitter pill to swallow, I realize. And the Truth is still the Truth. I know you are brave.

So now that you have had this swift and potent dose of the *'Truth'* about your Third Dimension, take heart to know that many Spiritual Devotees, some under My tutelage, use these newly acquired energies combined with aligned action, *to propel themselves onto the Fifth Dimension.*

The imbedded Human Spirit of adventure is an amazing positive force that focuses upon exploring the unknown, often for the betterment of Humanity. A Journey to Higher Dimensions is that of which I speak.

Always remember that *Free flowing engagement with willing passion* drives Devotees to excellence! Thus, We now move Our attention to the *Fifth Dimension of Higher Healing.*

The 5th Dimension

The House of Higher Healing

We Ascended Lovingly call this 5th Dimension a healing space that sources Love, harmony and abundance. Ones newly arriving will naturally vacillate a bit while transitioning upward between Dimensions, only to be reenforced and stabilized when resident in the 5th with overwhelming joy and gratefulness to finally know they have reached this point.

Ones describe their relief as 'feeling like a freed beast of burden'. They realize the vast quantities of life energies that have been sucked out of them to no avail, mind and body, ... by a life filled with judgements, opinions, being right, competition, placing blame, getting even, revenge and a host of other draining 3-D Ego behaviors.

In Gratefulness, Humans here in the 5th , ... awake and aware, *raise themselves* upward to heal. They ongoingly make Free-will choices embracing Love over the old rash Ego based thoughts, actions, and deeds of days and years gone bye. A leap forward beyond remarkable.

And yes, Devotees can slip occasionally, back into old patterns that are of necessity quickly realized and corrected … post haste… <u>through their own disciplinary Spiritual practice including a passion to grow and become One with Spirit.</u>

Kindly note, for Ones living in the 5th Dimension, it is common to occasionally 'float' back into the 3rd dimension, especially when discipline is temporarily lost over your Ego indulgence! Just pick yourself up,

recognize 'The Truth', and put in the *needed self-correction to regain the lost ground* ... and bring this maelstrom into focus. The maelstrom will become more clearly defined as you are living *in 5-D residence*, aware and awake now.

This refocusing and the *discipline to make change* is up to you. Dimensional climbers on the rise learn, beginning in the 3rd Dimension and solidifying in the 5th, to tell themselves 'The Truth' and adjust old habits accordingly. Recall that I mentioned earlier in the 3-D the *importance of how you process your Emotions?*

Contrary to certain popular Mystery school and religious teachings, Spirit does not do it for you. *Spirit does not make your choices or live your life for you.*

We Ascended Above will show you the way, and as your partners, and We will *guide you* to make wise choices along your healing path. Be crystal clear, however, that *choices are yours, and with you lies the responsibility for outcomes* as the chips fall where they may.

As in the 3-D, the same axiom applies here in the 5th, and beyond in the 7th and 9th Dimensions, I hasten to add!

To be sure, emotions will also keep flooding into 5th Dimensionals and beyond. The *difference for your vibration is how you processes them!* Emotions are a part of Human life. 9th Dimensionals have them too.

When you Master the discipline of processing your emotions (not stuffing) i n a Masterful manner, you have reached a pinnacle that opens your doors to compassion and Love.
Now can you see how this process is all coming together for you in the 5-D.

The choice replacing old habits with new habits of Self-Love is knocking at your door, here and now Folks. *What actions are you taking and what is your choice?*

Realize this about Self-correction. We Above will nudge you when correction is needed. It is *YOU who must accept the need for correctio*n as it arises, and then voluntarily *put* the healing in place in *your own* *consciousness*.

I know this question. Yes, certain burdens are ready, such Illusion and energies that realize the brings up an old We Ascended do lift from you when you as parts of the Human certain Karmic are balanced. But foundation for receiving all this *rests in your consciousness which you are responsible to manage and heal as I Am describing.*

> ***This is your journey, and you must walk the walk to stay on the crown of this road.***
>
> ***The 5th Dimension is an important rung on the Spiritual ladder upon which you must stand steadily in balance and then BE in residence.***

Mystery schools have been known to promote the myth that We Above do your Spiritual healings for you and all you have to do is show up and sit idly bye and 'hang out'. Nothing could be further from the Truth. This is a 3-D carrot to lure you in to take their bait.

There are no short cuts in this game, Folks. Spirit is not allowed to live your life for you or *to override your Free-will*. You create your own realities. We provide Wisdom and guidance for you to make Well-advised Free-will choices, and *YOU must make those choices of your own volition.* You will need to earn your own stripes, one by one. If you will surrender to Our spiritual coaching, this can *enable* your Dimensional vibration Ascension and You are thereby Blessed. Some, of course prefer to *go it alone* and *repeatedly fill their reserved seat on the Karmic wheel.*

The road gets narrower for you in the 5th, ... requiring constant vigilance and self-management of your process. Again, I Am available for consultation, and you must be available for *concentration, discipline and healing!* And then, concurrent satisfaction will come your way for life-lessons Well-learned and Mastered!

Often the UNIVERSE ITSELF will provide a 'sign' or a circumstance which gives you a timely sign. We Above will also give devoted Ones a tap to remind them when a self-correction is required to maintain 5th Dimensional residency!

Living in the 5th Dimension is tantamount to Being at *the base camp* at the foot of Mount Everest. You have made it this far, and now you must acclimatize to *this 5-D air*, soon to be rarer in Dimensions ahead.

Just to stay in residence here is your main concern, engaged in healings and enjoying the fruits of your Spiritual labors, which are quite delightful.

You will learn a new perspective about balancing your highs and lows and modulating energies, in daily practice. Entry into the 5th Dimension and *continued residency here, I must add, requires maintaining a delicate balance between, thought, action, and Karma.*

Ones entering this Dimension have earned their Spiritual stripes to be here and must hold this vibration by *consciously engaging in further needed Ego cleansing ... to maintain their spo*t on this new plateau, ... a higher reality without Human illusion ... a Divine territory that knows Universal Love, Self-love, and heartful dynamics of *all relationships ... not just during your lustful charades.*

An air of Oneness, joy, laughter, and celebration prevails. In this grand space of 'healing', you are gifted to experience new joys of simply being Human, embracing beauty, and experiencing ecstasy of erotic pleasures of heretofore unimaginable proportions for a Human, male, female (or not sure) ... *All are Blessed.* These experiences will intensify and carry on and endure in the higher Dimensions I Am addressing.

I speak of Divinely sourced pleasures for both the mind and body alike, ... states that emanate *in this higher vibration and beyond.* We Above call it Human - en – joy – ment, Folks!

The 5-D affords the opportunity to anchor those healed behaviors and thought patterns.

Be aware, Souls can rise into higher Dimensions in a single lifetime, ... or they can do so over

a time span of many many incarnations, lifetimes rotating upon the Karmic wheel.

When 5th Dimensionals in full residence have Mastered this level of vibration, they are candidates for the upcoming 7th Dimension about which I shall next speak.

৯ The 7ᵗʰ Dimension ৯

A Space of
Liberation and Being

This Divine space houses the elated vibration of Unconditional Love and Freedom. Everyday living with temptations for Ego judgements, anger or discordance can faintly be even recalled, much less contemplated or enacted. Joy is abundant.

Seventh Dimensional Ones Grace the Earth with their 'Beingness' in existential bliss of Unconditional Love. They have Mastered the giving of Unconditional Love carrying no need for its acceptance by others. This Divine *way of Being* will carry forward with these Ones into their 9ᵗʰ Dimensional level and beyond along housing the *manner* in which these Ones transmit their quantums of Light into spaces they can reach. In this Blessed 7ᵗʰ Dimension, these traits are gifts of the Heart, freely flowing outward from their gently pulsating Auras. Picture this if you will.

***Unconditional Love* has been inextricably imbedded.** It erases all traces of Ego energies, now fully and completely transcended. Anger and fear are neutralized in this energy field of the 7ᵗʰ· *Light prevails and Ascended*

Spirit will viscerally interact within them every minute of every hour of Earth time, awake or asleep.

Resistance to facing the Truth has evaporated, transmuted into enthusiastic heartful pursuit of uncovering exactly what is needed to reach win-win solutions and to put them into action. Harmony is thereby abundant! Emotions are processed with automaticity, ease and grace … without incident as before.

This manner of Being becomes a new modus operandi. It is automatic and carried out with joy, compassion and enthusiasm ... *which spreads to all living things around them.*

In the 7th, old discordant relationship dynamics have fully smoothed out. The emotions that plagued you in the 3-D and  sometimes as you were healing in the 5th-D … have all but dissipated in their importance. Your energies are now directed elsewhere. You will have assimilated and Mastered the guidance and teachings of My book, VICTORY FOR THE SOUL, *Relationships That Work*. (Amazon, Gordon Corwin II, Lah Rahn Ananda). It will have already become your bedside reference, along with Rising Up, I trust.

In this Dimension, You will automatically and effortlessly include in your dynamics key elements of timeless Truth, focused on creating Love and harmony in relationships *of all types.*

Here you *Lovingly embrace the reality of being fully liberated from the Human condition* ... such a grand milestone in your Spiritual journey. My congratulations to all 7th Dimensionals. New and enlightened behaviors have replaced those *old reactions* that created petty and devastating obstacles in your path.

However, before We go further, again here a word to the wise, a *word of caution:*

Divining Humans can, at times, imagine that they have leapt forward into an advanced Dimension, the 5th or 7th, or 9th, and they are still stuck somehow in a lower level. Segments of the Human *Condition,* ... here I speak of the Human *Illusion,* ... can strangely creep back into new Dimensional initiates, deluding them to believe they are an evolved someone they are not.

These are flashes of Ego remnants demanding recognition. A telltale giveaway of this delusion is when your behavior reflects this very illusion. At this point, Karma will step in. You will know. I will repeat this caution as well in My revelations about the 9th Dimension.

Alright.

We refer to the 7th as *the House of Being.* In this house, you have *a new version of Freedom* that eclipses all other known vibrations up to this point.

Once again, *now in residence at a higher level, you have been gifted with the release of a Human condition ...*

the burden of feeling shackled. With the Ascended Realm of Masters and Archangels at your side, … <u>you can now truly BE</u>.

Seventh Dimensional Souls have or will experience a *Soul merge,* … *such a Beloved part of this Grand Dimensional Process! This marvelous event marks a merge as One between the Soul and the Highest Self, the Grand Self as you sometimes say.*

7th Dimensionals are One.   One with each other, One with Spirit, and One with the Universe. Resistance that would say otherwise has faded into the past which cannot easily be recalled, I'm delighted to add. Oneness predominates in your vibration. It becomes contagious to those around you. *You are truly One with Spirit.*

A Soul Merge prepares Ones of this vibration to be magically swept away into higher etherical realms in due course. A harmony now plays its beautiful melody inward within your Being, and outward in your **Aura.**

An integrated Oneness of Being becomes a true reality.

This beautiful level of Being is also enabled by *Soul healings* taking place as a natural part of this elevated process. 7th Dimensionals experience Soul healings and cleansings of their *Soul element*s, … fractures, tears, and certain Karma.

Seventh Dimensional vibration Beings are on the threshold of total enlightenment. They are radiant, adorned with a brilliant aura *recognizable as pure joy* by the Kingdom  of Ascended Masters and Archangels … by other and Humans of Different Dimensions, … some higher and some lower. This way of recognizing and being recognized is akin to the Arcturian way … by vibration level, replacing facial features and physiognomy, for example.

Ones in the 7th witness and waft heightened aromas and flavours rarely available to other Humans.

Brilliant rays of silver light surround this primordial space, with radiant hues of silver, gold, yellow, violet, and pearl.   In this space of Being, … Unconditional Love is exclusively practiced together by all residents with automaticity and grace.

Ones holding this elevated space in their Personal Universe carry a beauteous aura that presents itself wherever they are, … wherever they go.

Their consciousness is smiling at themselves from the inside and smiling at others on the outside.

These Ones viscerally feel heightened unique mind and body sensations throughout … magnificent waves of energy about which they are fully conscious!

To be clear Folks, *living in this higher Dimension is a natural Super-Human phenomenon,* and certainly not to be confused with drug or alcohol induced illusions during sundry orgies that engulf the 3rd Dimensional Human condition. Have you been there recently?

I speak of a version of Oneness and Unconditional Love that knows true Divine reality in its grandest sense, ... *without pretense from Human illusion.* Love at this height is all consuming, with no reservations or conditions. In the 7th, this Unconditional Love is seen, felt, and always known ... throughout your days and nights alike.

Ones feel they have somehow drowned in euphoria, intoxicated with My elixirs and yet fully awake and aware ... if you can comprehend My irony.

A keen awareness of *the joys of Being Human* Rises Up, only to be topped by unending *Gratefulness.* I speak of Gratefulness for the sum of enlightenment reached thus far experienced in this lifetime, alive and living upon Earth.

Realize ... as I have aforementioned, ... *this escalation of Dimensions* may be attained in a single full lifetime incarnation or over several incarnation cycles. As I have also spoken, those who spin on the Karmic wheel and land incarnated upon Earth once again will be *inserted into the 3rd Dimension, only to start and resume the escalation once again.* Some who have previously come part way, say to the 7th, and then reincarnate again, can

easily move up the ladder again at a young age with ease and grace in their *own aligned process,* attaining previous higher levels and above.

As in the 3$^{rd\ and}$ 5th Dimensions, the Chakras of Ones in the 7th can also be balanced and cleansed and healed with daily regularity, through enlightened practices of the Tao combined with Ascended Realm touches delivered by Lord El Morya's Blessings. I mention this process here as it more often shows at this level, although also at lower Dimension levels for the fortunate.

In a sense, this is a *vibrational decontamination rinse,* orchestrated from Above for continuous daily and/or nightly Chakra energy center balancing … healing, purification and realignment, … gratis. During this process, energies move up and down the spine, pulsating along the spinal column, emanating from organs in the pelvic region, at times lasting for several minutes duration. When this unique neurological connection becomes *established,* healing Chi energy travels through the spinal column into the hypothalamus and pituitary glands in the Human brain. This phenomenon is achievable by Ones who have Mastered extreme body relaxation and breathing techniques and have full body control to start and maintain this process.

When thus connected in full synchronicity, this energy movement process starts muscle contractions and simultaneously ignites a rapid firing of brain neurons with extreme intensity, … as Chakra balancing occurs.

Human joys, of rarely known proportions of bliss and
ecstasy, are experienced during
this conscious/ semi-
conscious state. Full body
and mind sensations during
the process combined with
Love and healing are
inwardly passed to organs
within the body. Energies are
also passed to and from the
Ethers during this little-
known process.

While this *alchemical transmutation* is occurring, both
mental and physical sensations are keenly experienced.
Multiple sets of energy waves can continue for many
Earth- minute durations and then repeat. Heightened
energy waves pass out of the head and into the Chakra,
pleasingly stimulating scalp areas. Then, leaving the
Human body, the ultimate destination of this euphoric
energy stream is a return back into the Ethers and to Spirit
from whence it originally emanated ... a reverse
lightening rod of sorts.

This elevating phenomenon that I will refer to as
Chakragasma, ... *alters energies in Chakra centers* by
*injecting new and fresh rebalancing energy, with
simultaneous and* subsequent mental upliftment,
satisfaction, calmness and relaxation. Unfortunately, this
phenomenon is rarely experienced by Humans en mass.

A Being thus balanced daily ... is repeatedly neurologically <u>'re-booted'</u> ... as you would say, ... with a nervous system now refreshed ... 'Back to the factory settings', as God's true and balanced version of You, ... *to maintain and continue vibrat*ing joyfully with ease and grace ... and Chakras are once again in balance, ... for as long as they are. ... (Master chuckles).

Ones experiencing this Chakra balancing on a regular basis ... in concert with Transcendental Meditation, can likely maintain an ongoing inner peace and well-being ... heretofore unknown to them. Believe Me or not, this state can be *attained and* *lived* while incarnated in the flesh. This is not a 'pipe dream', I promise you. I speak Truth always. Those of you that attain this of level Chakra control will celebrate with Me in My crystal cave of Light with elixirs that titillate your senses, a part of a new level of Dimensional consciousness!

❧❧

Residents of the 7th Dimension have adopted at their core level a new Way of Being where emotions become a synchronous and now complementary part of living, wrapped in joy and Unconditional Love, and enthusiasm that is contagious.

With Soul Merge in place, living in this higher Dimension demonstrates a natural Super-Human phenomenon, ready for the final lap. <u>Few will recognize *themselves* as Ones of this level, yet others will plainly see.</u> *Seventh Dimensional vibrations tell the tale.*

Thus, elevated and stabilized in the 7th Dimension, and having taken full residence with existential bliss of Unconditional Love as a partner, ... these Ones are *candidates to be ushered into the highest octave of attainable Human consciousness, the Beloved 9th Dimension.*

This milestone marks your gigantic next step into the 9th Dimension and into the Ultimate Love Triangle.

<u>Spirit's Energies</u>

Your Consciousness   Relationships and
Inside your Personal Universe   Outside Circumstances

❧ The 9th Dimension ❧

Palace of Purity

The Ninth Dimension of Human consciousness houses Beloved Ones of Universal purity, the ultimate pinnacle for an *incarnated* Human.

This Grand level of Being **brilliantly radiates elevated vibrations now purified to the highest Human octave.**

Ninth Dimensionals extend energies into vast reaches far around the Earth Globe and into the Cosmos, *vibrating in unison* with the planes of Masterful and Angelic Kingdoms, and often with other Worlds in the Earth's vast solar system. Beloved Ninth Dimensionals continue serving upon Earth, and all the while dancing in rhythm with consciousnesses of Great Spirit and the Universe.

Yes, this is a Super-human calling, and it is answered by these Ones anointed by Spirit who selflessly radiate copious vibrational quantities of Wisdom, Love and joy.

This level of evolvement is truly at the threshold of Super-Human. We in Spirit crown all who have arrived at this

new residence Universe. This reflect eons of incarnations, foundation incarnated blossom and for their Personal attainment may multiple Earthly constructed on a enabling an lifetime to bloom into full enlightenment.

Perpetually effervescing Unconditional Love is a grand characteristic that marks 9ᵗʰ Dimensionals as their true way of Being. *Remarkably* similar to magnificent Pleiadean evolvement in this extremely high place of Being, … <u>9ᵗʰ *Dimensionals fully embody and Master the giving of true Unconditional Love with no expectation of acceptance.*</u>

Witnessing the presence of this and endless more pinnacles of vibration of 9ᵗʰ Dimensional Ascension can be ultimately heartwarming if not breathtaking … for you who now climb the Spiritual ladder. *Unconditional Love is nested in these Ones* <u>still holding a natural state of Being.</u>

As regards the heart space of Unconditional Love in particular, Pleiadean Beings are known to be roughly fifty thousand years advanced beyond your 3ʳᵈ Dimensional Earth society. Extrapolate for yourself, if you will, to the pinnacle level reached by incarnated 9ᵗʰ Dimensional Earthly Beings whom I praise here and now! <u>*In this particular respect,*</u> their consciousness sits on a par with Love Masters of the Pleiadean World. Enough said.

The achievement of *reaching and residing* in this 9ᵗʰ Dimension is an Extra-ordinary Human achievement of the highest order. We anoint Ones holding this vibration with laurels and garlands of praise. You are examples of culminated Extra-ordinary lifetimes as gargantuan achievements of Super-human proportions. You are here, cum laude!

And to ensure balance in this mix, **I repeat again a word of caution for My readers.** Beware of <u>Ego delusions</u> that would somehow convince yourself that you have miraculously been thrusted Above … skipping many required rungs on the Spiritual ladder, … only now to be miraculously ripped from your 3rd Dimensional seat and now suddenly plunked into the 9th Dimension … as a Being of the highest order! (Master chuckles …)

<u>Dimensionals of the 9th have earned their spots</u>. They are frequently called upon by Spirit to pass and receive communications from other Worlds, the Pleiades, Orion, and Venus in particular. They serve Humanity to learn more while this Universal window of space and time is open as it is.

Unseen by the masses, these gifts of etherical *Love and Gratefulness abound* here in the 9th. Infusions of energy from the Ascended Realms ongoingly populate the

consciousness of 9th Dimensional Ones. As instruments of Spiritual nourishment to Mankind, they in turn pass through and deliver an abundance of Love downward throughout the lesser Dimensions I describe to you. Somewhat akin to elder brothers and sisters of Wisdom.

Divine assignments and duties begin to take precedence, while collateral Earthly responsibilities, still honored, fade softly into the background.

We Ascended give Spiritual assignments to 9th Dimensionals, extending their arms further outward. As an example of this, We have been known to delegate authority and responsibility to the hands of 9th Dimensionals of Spirit for placing one or more Legions of Angels in service. Under their care, *Angels are dispatched to deserving locations* as known and intuited by the 9th Dimensionals themselves.

These actions involve assignment of Angelic Pods to specific tasks befitting to Divinely assist deserving Humans of aligned merit.

An Angel Pod is comprised of 12 Angel energy quantums, and 12 Pods make up one Legion. The sum being a massive quantum of 144 points of Angelic energy thereby assembled.

Angelic energy Pods may be dispatched by selected 9th -D representatives of Ourselves, … as various Spiritually worthy needs of Humans present themselves around your globe ... a Spiritual mechanism tantamount to *Earthly perceptions of answered prayers.*

As these and other Divine assignments are carried out, Ones charged with delivering such Divine duties are concurrently overcome with joy, ecstatic with relief to finally be <u>Free.</u>

On behalf of Humanity, these *Fully Enlightened* 9-D Beings also transmit and receive unique energies, functioning as a valuable bridge between Worlds, and yet they are still embodied.

Theses Souls of the 9th Dimension are *semi-Ascended Beings*. Surprisingly to many of you, they remain incarnated in the flesh, unpretentiously dressed in plain clothes. Does this surprise you?

While thus remaining incarnated upon Earth, these

Purified Ones have already begun to serve in other Masterful capacities, preparatory to elevated various assignments higher up under My tutelage *Unconditional Love is nested in these Ones* still holding a natural state of Being.

We Above retain some certain 9-D Ones thus serving in place on Earth, while others are Lovingly Transitioned into Spirit under Our wings.

In a Human lifetime, this retention is extra-ordinary.

Such a state of peacefully Being Human **was intended** to inhabit natives when your species was created. Earthlings were tested early in the evolutionary chain to see how they would individually and collectively *choose to use their gift of Free-will.*

The outcome of this choice was and is what you now see in front of you as the 3rd Dimension.

We Above intend to source an extraordinary healing of *Humanity's use of Free-will* …to bring back and fully restore the consciousness originally intended upon Creation.

The Angelic Realm, about which I shall next speak, is inextricably bonded with the Realm of Ascended Masters, delivering never ending quantums of Light into the collective and individual vibrations which pervade this Earth in this Age.

The 10ᵗʰ Dimension

Where Angels Tread

A nd now, We shall journey further beyond. I bring these next Love-laden words to you in quiet serenity. Entry into this Domain marks the *shifting of Human Energies of the incarnated into Heavenly energies of the Ascended.*

Expanding into a Cosmic Dimension, We unveil to you a unique grouping of Ascended energy Beings who dwell in the 10th Dimension. They tenderly deliver their unique touch bearing the Light of Unconditional Love … their endless uplifting service to Mankind, … and a tireless Angelic dedication to blending with the Ascended Master realm in seamless synchronicity for Divine purpose.

These delicate yet powerful energies insert their *gifts of Light* into heart-spaces, Human consciousnesses and their inevitable circumstances upon Earth. Their presence is *able to be experienced by some of you as incarnated Humans, and yet they dance in their unique Angelic vibration … one unattainable by you while incarnated in the flesh.*

A simple touch by Angelic Beings is indeed a delightful, comforting, reassuring and heartwarming event whenever and wherever it may grace you. Deeply welcome and appreciate in gratefulness your contacts with these 10th Dimensional servants of Humanity, Folks. A single touch from your Guardian Angel marks a magnificent Blessing of honor. On a larger scale, a touch from a Pod or Legion of Angels will re-boot your life, or lift you up and through a difficult circumstance … folding Grace into your very Being! I trust some of you have experienced this Blessing.

I also trust you will always hold an 'Angel's touch' in *true Gratefulness of Heart* … as Our Beloved Quan Yin has so eloquently expressed.

Angelic Beings are recognizable by *feeling their vibrational presence* and or by their *colors*, vague as they might be. You would not recognize them draped with Earthly clothes of flamboyant regalia or as miniature naked infant bodies shown in religious scenes for mass Human consumption.

These Etherical energies, as Angels, Pods and Legions of Love and Light are recognizable *by their vibrations and auras*. *If you have the gift, they can be felt or seen by the Human eye on the fringe of ultra-violet spectrum perception.*

Alright.

Perhaps you have experienced being touched by Angels? Being awake and aware in their proximity is indeed a *mesmerizing personal experience* of delight along your Spiritual journey.

So, when you feel an Angels's touch, take a deep breath and relax your curiosity Ego, drift into a wistful space of surrender … bask in the wondrousness of this *joyful energy*, … and know you are touched with Grace.

Paramount for you is to have a keen sense of this Angelic Realm and of their delicate Loving touch … and of the *uplifted by assistance they can be to you in resolving Human circumstances along your path.*

Earthly religions call the *inexplicable handiworks of Angelic presences* to be inexplicable 'miracles', while

We above would describe an *Angels touch as Divine synchronicity showered downward by Our Grace for the Higher Good.* Perhaps you have experienced that of which I speak?

At each Blessed touch, you will be wise to respond with *abundant Gratitude*, expressed silently or aloud as you will. The Angels can feel you. Your expressed gratefulness, silently or aloud, is known and always received by all parts of the Angelic Kingdom.

On a Grand level, Ascended Master Archangel Michael presides over the Angelic Kingdom and its Legions, co-sourcing the First Ray of Spirit alongside Beloved Master El Morya ... both holding this Blue Ray, the Will of God,

~ CONCLUSION ~

S pirit has for eons been contacting the Human collective and sourcing individual Ones who are ready to engage in the evolvement of consciousness, *Rising Above* to higher Dimensions of opportunity, healing, Unconditional Love, and purity, as I have revealed in this discourse.

The ultimate outcome of evolvement *for incarnated Humans* is to reach the 9th Dimension. This rise may come to reality over a span of one or more lifetime incarnations.

The Dimensional Ascension process commences in the 3rd Dimension where Humans reincarnate, and then progressively escalates, ... if they choose ... by thought, action and deed ... upward to the 5th, 7th, and 9th Dimensions. Each level above the 3rd Dimension marks a major rung in the Spiritual ladder of Ascension, *ever present to be climbed and held in residence until Mastered.*

In your hands You now hold a Divinely sourced Wisdom- filled presentation of the Dimensions that potentially lie along your road ahead, depending upon your Free-will choices.

Your dedication, passion, grit, and perseverance will be tested to the hilt in becoming the Extraordinary evolved Being that yearns to be purified, Free and One with Spirit.

Always remember to watch your step and to walk caringly upon the crown of this ever-narrowing road, with your Loving focus resolutely centered in aligned purpose.

We Ascended Above realize the difficulty of releasing your Ego-based attachments. Clinging to Ego behavior and it's baggage is a common 3rd Dimensional instinct in lower Dimensions of consciousness that grips vast Human multitudes. When you reach Higher Dimensions, you will have had to give up many old, precious, and worn-out Ego parts of You ... in order to step out and step up to a higher Dimension.

As Maha Chohan of this Aquarian Age, I Lovingly Bless each of you who truly engage in this process of Grand Dimensional Ascension. Join Me in My crystal Cave of Light as you Rise Above and graduate into higher Dimensions of Being. We shall exuberantly celebrate in unison and Oneness the milestone victories you achieve and anchor as yours forever.

My energies of Gratefulness outflow to All who are consciously engaging in the Beloved process of Dimension Ascension into Higher planes. As willing and devoted participants who fully engage, showing 063

immeasurable courage to continuously pursue Super-human feats, ... I join with You to bring forth the Light of your inborn Christ consciousness into Being.
I Bless you in the Highest.

I congratulate All of those who garner the courage, Self-Love, and energies of heart, mind, body and consciousness to stay the continuing course in this Grand Dimensional Ascension Process. You are All honored in highest and lovingly held in grand esteem in the arms of the Ascended Kingdoms of Masters and Archangels joined as One.

I Bless you always

Saint Germain

And Gordon Corwin II aka Lah Rahn Ananda

QUOTATIONS

FROM

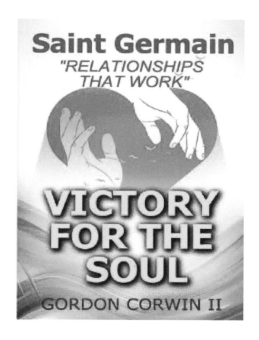

Awareness

Gaining *awareness* *is the first step in your liberation from the Human Illusion.*

Notice the sense of Freedom that you can generate when your priority

fits the need!

❧❧

Partnership

A confluent overlap of Consciousnesses between partners is a beautiful
blending of energies sourcing a true relationship to be born,
blossom, and thrive.

In Partnership, as in Your Own Grand Process, the middle or the end
may or may not faintly resemble the beginning ... as Change has its
way!

Celebrate and embrace your shared Love, life's lessons learned, and
Win-Win outcomes ... that you create together as 'Us' in relationship.

About Desire, ... Truly *Being* in full-hearted, flourishing relationship is for Ones with commitment, and the faint of heart need look elsewhere.

Trust in Spirit when We say that
beyond your comfort zone
lies the space of evolved growth
and its potential rewards.

The power of enlightened teamwork and bonding, through a mindset of Us and We, is a trustable asset to anchor relationships of all types.

As surely as individuals make up their partnership in union, they can also maintain their own *appropriate* individual identities.

Perception

Let it be said that We are all bonded together as One in the grandest sense, albeit as Beings now in Ascended Spirit, or as you are now incarnated in the flesh.

When Bonding is *intensified into a tightly held forever-binding* Attachment ... never ever to escape your clutch and grasp, ... know that you are obsessed and Bound!

The *'compromise', as a well-worn out solution*, is so common in your World, yet so deeply impregnated with an Earth-World consciousness that buys this Human Illusion as its flawed truth.

Being left dissatisfied or in emotional limbo casts its own shadow on the compromise just reached, even though 'agreed' upon.

Do your level best to take lifetime experiences and their outcomes in stride.

Drink the nectar from your life's lessons, Drop by Drop.

Patience

Moreover, *for Advanced Spiritual Beings* on the Earth plane, indulgence in anger-filled reactions is now an <u>Ego luxury</u> that you can ill afford.

You are wise from this moment forward to consider patience as <u>mandatory,</u> not an optional frivolity of your relationship.

Are you going to stay stuck INSIDE the upset or choose now to stand OUTSIDE of the upset   viewing its reflection from a new perspective?

Patience is the catalyst that allows space for creation of Win-Win solutions!

Patience is needed for *Divine Timing* to incubate.

In the end, when all is said and done, allow yourself the joys of remembering the finest relationship moments you shared, holding them dearly in Gratitude, as flames of eternal Love, alive and well.

આ⁀ઙ

Change

Change will have *Its Way, regardless.*

Being a Friend of Change will strengthen you in facing the inevitable.

Freely Allowing Change as it pops up in your life,
is an attribute of consciousness for a person committed and
empowered to pursue an examined Human Lifetime,
leading to the ExtraOrdinary!

Change can be viewed from a number of different perspectives, as your consciousness and Ego will allow.

On the brighter side, changing times can be often welcomed by some as a refreshing manifestation of the new, beyond the Status Quo!

৵৽৻

Ego

Egos will try their best to hold you prisoner in the illusion that 'you are <u>always</u> right'.

The grizzly ingredients of an upset on fire within will easily fuel the 'always right Ego on duty'.

There is a high ransom, indeed, that Human Spirit of potential needs to
pay for the
stubborn and resolute
self-indulgences of Narcissism.

Your Ego can hold you captive, shackled in its prison, if you choose.

Relationship Mastery requires discovering those default responses,
packed tightly in your belief system, that will surely need to be
jettisoned while your Ego must pay the price of submission!

Resistance or surrender ... your obstacle or your miracle?

As a captive of your Ego,
your hands are tied.

Egos are reluctant if not deaf to the naked truth.

Resistance is a costly chosen behavior when choice of Truth comes knocking!

~›‌›

Truth and Illusion

Let you not always dignify *your experience* as the absolute truth of the matter!

Opinions are only Opinions*!*

Illusion is at odds with the Truth and it is the grand disguise that covers up!

Truly and fully *knowing yourself* disarms self-deception and denial.

છન્≪

Self-talk Self-Love

Being Truth is Self-Love.

Self-love leads you to find Peace within yourself.

Celebrate and embrace your shared love,
life's lessons learned, and Win-Win outcomes ... that you create
together.

And, where Love is yearned for, perhaps it magically appears for you
as the place you have longed to enter ... and you wonder why it has

And, where Love is yearned for, perhaps it magically appears for you as the place you have longed to enter ... and you wonder why it has

A healthy Self-talk dialogue can sing delightfully to the highest octave of your consciousness and make you smile, inside and out.

Be brutally honest with yourself about purifying your Self-talk thoughts, as Self-dishonesty results in an Ego deceiving a fool. Both are wasting their time!

In a sense your Self-Talk defines a large part of who you really are at the core level.

Similar to shifting *Judgements into Non-Judgement*s ... shifting *Attachment into Detachment is equally impactive ...* when translated into Detachment with Love.

Once a delicate perspective of Balance is achieved
in some degree of Mastery,
happiness flows into the mixture
like honey from the hive you have created!

৵৽

Emotions

Trust in Spirit when We say that
beyond your comfort zone lies the space of evolved growth

with its potential rewards.

To heal the *effect* of your own 'Triggers' is to heal the vibration of your

own Emotions.

The *One* who becomes angry has become a captive of their own
device!

Master your Emotions, and you can become a
Blessed Spiritual Observer
beyond the reach of Earthly anxieties.

Let the Emotions of Others be theirs
Without obligation
To make them yours.

Communication

Put Ambiguity aside, Dear Ones,
And make your communications
Clear, crisp, and well-considered
Before your mouth shall have its way.

One face of you turns out to be the way you communicate.

Building Communication *skill*
Requires attention to your choice of words, and a focus upon their
delivery
Where actions match your communications!

You can be Master of clear communications or let your communication
breakdowns be the
Master of you.

Communicating from the Heart in authentic Relationship delivers an
even exchange of energy, positive and with Love.

ठ∼∽

Love, Compassion, and Forgiveness

Remember, Receiving is also part of the Grand Process, *and* you are divinely entitled to receive when alignment, gratitude and Love are yours!

Choosing actions that generate Love, happiness and Soul growth for others opens the portal for
The same energy flowing back unto you
... In kind!   Divine Reciprocity.

Half-assed approaches to relationship rarely bear the fruit.

Saint Germain Quotations

From previous channelings

Keen are the uses of adversity.

Develop the ability to discern without the
burden of Ego's judgements being inserted into the mix.

Surrender Yourself to Truth and Reality without compromising
intention.

Left and right together join the absolute and the relative.

Dig deeply for rewards of the Truth.

Willingly abide with the Truth about things and people ... without judegment ... and know Freedom.

Acknowledge Reality and engage in its uses.

Giving True Unconditional Love requires there be no expectation of acceptance.

Saint Germain

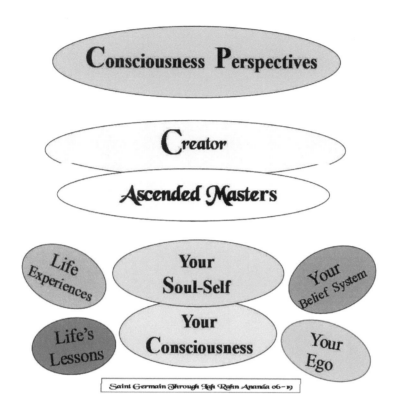

Consciousness Perspectives

Creator

Ascended Masters

Life Experiences

Your Soul-Self

Your Belief System

Life's Lessons

Your Consciousness

Your Ego

Saint Germain Through Jah Rahn Ananda 06-19

DISCLAIMER

The information contained within this Book is strictly for educational purposes. This Book and the Book's elements are provided to readers committed to Spiritual education, self-discovery, self-actualization, and transformation to align individual belief systems with a common source, Our Creator and Spirit, as the guiding light to enter doorways of change, new possibilities, growth, and manifestations within reach of an extraordinary and self-examined Human lifetime. Readers are encouraged to choose, of their own free- will and volition, to accept, to follow, or to reject the guidance, ideas, philosophies, stated truths, and techniques presented herein. If you wish to apply ideas and guidance contained herein, you are taking full responsibility for your actions. This Book contains information and general advice that is intended to help the readers to be better informed about physical, mental, emotional, and Spiritual wellbeing. Always consult your doctor for your individual needs. This Book is not intended to be a substitute for the medical advice of a licensed physician. The reader should consult with their doctor in any matters relating to his/her health. This Book contains information and general advice about business pursuits. This book is not intended to be a substitute for financial or legal advice. Reader is advised to consult your licensed financial or legal professional for such matters. In no event does the author or the publisher make guarantees, express or implied, as to results or consequences arising out of or related to the reader's use or inability to use the book's contents. Both the author and Highland Light Publishers (the publisher) do not assume and hereby disclaim any liability to any party for any loss, direct, indirect, or consequential damages, accidental, unintentional, or unforeseen, pain, suffering, emotional distress, or disruption resulting from the reader's negligence, actions or non-actions, accident, or any other cause.

About the Author

ordon Corwin II, also known as Lah Rahn Ananda, translated literally as 'God Light Messenger', is a native Californian, educated at UC Berkeley, followed by service as a Commissioned US Naval Officer, and by extensive careers in the computer and real estate industries.

In 1995, Gordon clearly heard Lord Saint Germain's resounding and mysterious voice from Above, recruiting him to immediately engage with Ascended Spirit and follow his Soul's calling to reactivate his considerable past life Atlantean DNA channeling abilities, and to begin walking his Dharma to serve Humanity!

As an appointed Masters' Representative, Lah Rahn then began delivering Ascended energies through channeling of the Masters' words and visual media, which would now become his changed and conscious life path. In 1998 he founded The Light of the Soul Foundation, a qualified non-profit entity for advanced Spiritual education and Human philanthropy.

084

Following years of ego-cleansing by the Masters, Lah Rahn Ji has, for 25 years now, delivered clear and engaging channelings of public and private Spiritual events along with potent and enlightening mentoring of Chelas in The Light of the Soul Vortex in Southern California. In 2007 he was highly honored to be chosen by Lord Saint Germain to be the Ascended Masters' instrument and Partner to begin, and later complete, this precise and accurate channeling to Earth of The Saint Germain Chronicles Collection, A Journey Into Practical Spirituality 2008-2014. In 2020 Lah Rahn again partnered with Saint Germain to write Victory For The Soul, Relationships that Work, among other published channelings along with those from Quan Yin and El Morya.

Lah Rahn aka Gordon Corwin currently lives in Oceanside, California and is available for private channelings and group events, as well as public speaking engagements.

Contact:
GordonCorwin24@gmail.com
Lah@SaintGermainChronicles.com

Light of the Soul
Foundation
Established 1998

The Light of the Soul Foundation is a Charitable non-profit
501 (c) (3) Philanthropic Organization founded in 1998 by
Gordon Corwin, Trustee.

This non-denominational Foundation is dedicated to

The Spiritual Enlightenment of Humanity.

LOSF continues to be harmoniously bonded with

Highland Light Publishers,

sharing this Spiritual mission that includes writing, publishing
and distributing Masters' books in addition to delivering live
events with wisdom from The Ascended Masters Above.

"Bringing the Light of Spirit into the *every-day lives* and
consciousness of the masses
in an increasingly troubled earthly world
… is the practical gift We lovingly offer".

As you now may observe, the collective behavior of Humanity
continues pervasive behaviors that prevail without change.

Your kind philanthropy, donations, and bequests provide the
financial means enabling Us to continue serving and delivering
Enlightenment from Above, expanding Our outreach of Light.

Your donations transform Ones aspiring to reach
and live their full Dharma's potential of Love
awareness, Compassion and Soul evolvement …
which calls to Humanity in these pivotal times.

Light of the Soul Foundation

Charitable **Non-profit 501 (c) (3)**

Public Events and Spiritual Counseling

 **EIN: 91-1945098**

**For Your Gifts, Donations, or Bequest Confirmations,
By Check, Credit Card or Wire:**

We are deeply grateful to Donors, Contributors and
Philanthropists for your fine and generous *Gifts of Grace
to uplift The Human Consciousness.*

You are an
immensely essential resource that ongoingly empowers
Our continuing Outreach.

For two decades, We have delivered gifts of
Soul Enlightenment and Practical Spirituality via
recently published channeled works, along with public
events and   Spiritual readings … with your generous
support!

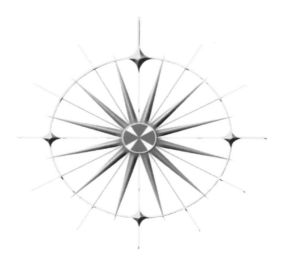

Light of the Soul Foundation
(501)(c)(3)

www.SaintGermainChronicles.com

EIN: 91-1945098

CPSIA information can be obtained
at www.ICGtesting.com
Printed in the USA
BVHW022029050922
646268BV00001B/1